This Little
PIGGY

THE TALE OF AN EXTRAORDINARY PIGGY BANK

JAC ARBOUR

PROCEEDS
PRESS

This Little Piggy
by Jac Arbour

Published by ProⒸeeds Press, LLC
Hallowell, Maine 04347

ISBN: 978-0-9898927-2-8
Library of Congress Control Number: 2020923978

Edited by Dan Koon and Shellie Braeuner
Copy edited by Amy Chamberlain
Cover and book design by Carrie Cook
Cover and interior illustrations by Kalleheikki Kannisto

For more information,
including the philanthropic mission of ProⒸeeds Press,
please visit www.jacarbour.com

Printed in the USA

First Edition
1 3 5 7 9 10 8 6 4 2

Dedicated to today's youth,
for their unique differences,
their big dreams,
their extraordinary potential,
and all the good they will do
for this world

CONTENTS

INTRODUCTION   ix

CHAPTER 1: The Blue Ribbon & the Long Walk Home   1

CHAPTER 2: The Founder of Pennyville   9

CHAPTER 3: May the Journey Begin   17

CHAPTER 4: Tenfold   23

CHAPTER 5: We All Have Needs   31

CHAPTER 6: Pay Yourself First   39

CHAPTER 7: We All Have Wants   45

CHAPTER 8: We All Have Desires   53

CHAPTER 9: Do the Right Thing   61

CHAPTER 10: The Fourth Slot   69

CHAPTER 11: The Last Three Pennies   79

CHAPTER 12: True Wealth   87

ACKNOWLEDGEMENTS   91

INTRODUCTION

Firmly rooted in the rolling hills of northern New England is a small town known as Pennyville. It is a unique town that is flourishing today because of something wonderful that happened there many years ago.

Back when Pennyville was founded, the residents agreed to take a certain approach to life: First, all folks agreed that there is incredible value in focusing on the well-being of others. So, placing the well-being of others first is exactly what they did. Second, they decided to make achieving happiness—*true* happiness—the motivation behind their every word and action. So, they did things—big things and small things—that would make themselves and those around them truly happy: from paying a compliment to a stranger, to going out of their way to help a friend in need. In this small town, this approach to life continues to this day. It has become a way of life that not only benefits everyone in Pennyville, but it ripples into surrounding communities, making a lasting impression on all who experience it.

The citizens of Pennyville are likely "different" from anyone in your town. The folks in Pennyville come in all shapes, sizes, and colors—some with two feet and some with four. Regardless, they all treat one another the same: with respect. By having respect for one another, the residents of Pennyville have made their town a place where diversity is welcome, and everyone's contributions are appreciated.

The young citizens of Pennyville learn early on that every one of them has unique strengths due to their differences. Truly, there is no reason for anyone in this town (or, really, anywhere) to feel strange, or insecure, or to feel the need to change something about him- or herself in order to fit in, for the truth is, we were all made to stand out.

The story that follows is about Philip Anthropist, a young piglet growing up in the extraordinary town of Pennyville. Early in the story, we see Philip's feelings crushed by the cruel words and actions of outsiders. Philip originally feels embarrassed and ashamed of his differences. Hurt by the cruel words of others, Philip believes things might be easier, more enjoyable, and ultimately more rewarding, if he were exactly *the same* as at least some of the other animals he knew.

Just when he is feeling truly hopeless, Philip picks up an unusual friend who helps him begin to discover, for himself, some interesting truths about his family history, about the founder of Pennyville, and about the benefits of being unique. It is only then that Philip begins to understand and then embrace his differences and, finally, set hoof on his own path to happiness and things larger—much larger—than himself.

Chapter 1

THE BLUE RIBBON &
THE LONG WALK HOME

Philip's hooves pounded as he flew down the street.

"Nyah, nyah!"

"Four Slots!"

Voices called out from just a short distance behind. Philip was trying to outrun them.

The little pig turned a corner and saw the Pennyville Town Hall shining bright and white in the afternoon sun. The offices would be closed—everyone was at the fair. Philip could only hope the back doors were left unlocked.

Please be open! Please be open! Philip thought as he ran up the steps.

Philip grabbed the handles and swung the doors open, then looked behind him as they fell closed. He didn't see the group who was chasing him.

He felt safe. Philip heaved a sigh of relief.

And the day had been going so well.

The corn-eating contest at the county fair had just ended. Philip had trained to compete for weeks. Then, when he ate that last piece of corn, held up his hooves, and looked to his left and right, he was so surprised he hardly heard the judge call out, "The winner!"

Philip thought he would burst with joy when they pinned the blue ribbon onto his shirt.

But that's when it started.

"Four Slots!"

"Loser!"

Philip glanced down and saw Bradly, the young badger, with his gang behind him. Ronnie, a raccoon, was pulling his mouth into silly faces while the raven named Rachel flapped over the crowd screeching, "Loser!"

Philip tried to ignore the kids calling him names. But, just as soon as he left the stage, they started throwing mud at him, which isn't something you can ignore.

Running seemed like his best option.

And that had brought him here, with his pink ear against the big wooden doors, listening.

Then he heard Bradly's voice close by: "I think he ran, whee, whee, whee, all the way home."

"Good one, Bradly," said Rachel.

Philip heard Ronnie's loud chuckle. Bradly and his friends were always picking on him. This group of three ruled the playground, and they never let Philip forget that he was different from the other animals in town.

He was even different from every other pig he knew.

The voices got softer as the gang went on their way.

Leaning with his back against the door, Philip breathed a huge sigh of relief, sliding down the door until he was sitting. He just wanted to rest here, alone in the cool, dark, empty building.

At least he thought he was alone.

"Something wrong?"

Philip looked up to see Mr. Webber. The old turtle leaned on his cane and looked over his glasses with a kind expression.

"No," Philip quickly replied, looking everywhere except at Mr. Webber's face.

"Hmm," said Mr. Webber. "Well, it's good to see you, Philip. Come with me."

Philip could hardly say no. He got up from the floor and followed the turtle, winding through the dark halls of Town Hall until they reached the front lobby. Floor-to-ceiling windows bathed the room with light, chasing the shadows away. In the brightest patch of light hung a painting. It was the portrait of the founder of Pennyville.

Philip stopped and looked at the painting of an elderly pig. The pig was wearing a gray tweed suit that matched the gray hair around his ears. In his arms, he held a big book with a red cover.

Mr. Webber stopped to look at the picture and sighed.

"Did you know that I knew him?" Mr. Webber asked.

"Isn't that the founder of Pennyville? And you knew him?" Philip asked. Then he added, "How old *are* you?"

"Old enough to remember the time before Pennyville," Mr. Webber chuckled. "Old enough to remember meeting Philip the First as a young pig full of ideas and with only a penny to his name."

Philip looked at the picture and tried to imagine the old boar as a young pig like himself. Then he noticed a little brass plaque under the portrait: "Philip Anthropist."

"Wait, he has the same name as me!"

"That's because, my young piglet, he is your great-great-great-grandsire."

"Really? You mean, I'm in the same family as him?"

"Yes," said Mr. Webber. "And you have something else in common."

"What?"

"He had four slots too."

Stunned, Philip just stood there and blinked.

"I promise you. He did," Mr. Webber said. Then, suddenly turning away, he added, "Maybe you should tell him about your day." The old turtle slowly made his way off into the shadows of the hallway.

Philip looked up at the picture of the grand old pig.

"Tell him about my day? It's not like he can hear me," Philip said aloud. But then again, when he looked carefully, the portrait's eyes seemed to be somehow twinkling in the sunlight.

"Anyway," Philip said, looking down and inspecting his hooves. "I bet you didn't really have four slots in your back. I bet Mr. Webber just said that to make me feel better."

When he looked up, Philip's mouth dropped in surprise.

The pig in the painting had turned around! Now, instead of his front, Philip the First's back was showing and, motionless, he was smiling over his shoulder.

Right there, in the middle of the older pig's back, were four pockets, one for each slot.

Just like Philip's!

Philip blinked and shook his head, not believing what he

saw. When he looked again, Philip the First was facing forward just as he had been before.

But there was one big difference.

Now his arms were empty. The big book was gone.

Philip's eyes immediately caught something glinting in the sun. There on the floor was the old book. It had fallen right out of the picture!

Philip bent over to inspect it. Printed in gold letters on the front cover were these words:

The word "Book" was large and centered in the middle of the cover. The book looked old, like something that should be in a glass case in a museum.

Like something he shouldn't touch.

"Mr. Webber!" Philip called. He waited for the old turtle to reappear.

But no one came.

I can't leave it here on the floor, Philip thought.

He reached out and touched the red leather cover. It felt warm to the touch. He picked the book up, expecting it to be heavy, but it was much lighter than he had thought. He hugged it to his chest.

"I'll take it home, just for tonight," Philip spoke directly to the painting. "I'll figure out what to do with it tomorrow."

While Philip looked up at the picture of his great-great-great-grandsire he thought he saw the old pig wink.

Chapter 2

THE FOUNDER OF PENNYVILLE

P hilip ran all the way home, holding the book close to his chest.

"Mom!" he called when he burst into their barn. There was no answer.

Philip trotted to his bedroom at the back of the barn and tossed the book toward his bed. The book fell open midair, and its pages splayed against the bedspread.

"Ouch!" said a muffled voice from the bed.

Philip stopped.

"You're going to break my spine!" the voice continued.

"What . . . ?"

"Is that any way to treat a book?" The book raised itself upright and faced Philip, blinking the two O's in "Book" just like eyes.

Philip inched over to the bed, poked the book, and jumped back.

"OW!" the book exclaimed.

"What are you doing?" Philip asked.

"I could ask you the same thing," said the book, settling itself against the pillows.

"I've never had a book ask me *anything* before," said Philip. "I mean," he added, "books don't talk."

"Of course they do," the book said. "Every book has something to say. Maybe you just haven't been listening."

"No, I know books *say* things, but . . . ," Philip started.

"But you just said you've never heard a book talk before."

Philip didn't know how to answer, so he asked, "What's your name?"

"I'm the Big Red Book," the book said, opening its pages and waving them at Philip.

"It says that on your cover," replied Philip, "but what's your *name*?"

"I'm THE Big Red Book," the book said. "I don't need another name."

"Umm, okay," said Philip.

"What's *your* name?"

"Philip."

"Oh," the book said. "Just like my writer."

"You mean my great-great-great-grandsire?" Philip asked, carefully counting out the "greats" on his hoof as he said them.

"He said I was one of the most valuable things in his life."

"Why is that?" Philip asked. "I thought he was rich and had lots of expensive things."

"There's more than one kind of wealth," the book said.

"I'm going to be rich when *I* grow up," Philip said.

The book sighed, closing its pages. "That's my job," it said. "I help animals build wealth."

"How so?" Philip asked. "If I were rich," he said, still thinking about earlier, "nobody would make fun of my four slots. Those bullies would have to be nice to me. Can you help me get rich?"

"Sure," the book sighed again. "You've got four slots. You could be just like Philip the First—or Phil, as I liked to call him," the book said.

"How?"

"There's really only one way to start becoming wealthy," the book said, looking around Philip's bedroom. His pages ruffled.

"Yeah?" Philip got excited. He couldn't wait to hear the answer. He was ready for the secret to getting rich. He leaned closer.

The book suddenly slammed its cover shut.

"I know you're a pig," the Big Red Book said. "But do you have to live in a pigsty?"

"What?" Philip was thrown off by the change of topic. "What does that have to do with getting rich?"

"Everything," the book said. "This room is a mess."

"Sure, there are some toys on the floor . . . ," Philip admitted.

"And socks on the desk." The book sniffed the air. "And they smell dirty."

Philip grabbed the socks and tossed them into his hamper. He shoved a pile of toys under his bed.

"Better?" Philip asked, flopping on the bed.

"Not really," the book said, turning its back cover toward Philip. "My writer never would have founded Pennyville with that kind of work ethic."

"What's 'work ethic'?" Philip asked.

"Phil-iip . . ." Philip's mother was calling him.

"I've got to go," Philip said, turning toward the door. Then he stopped. "You aren't going anywhere, are you?"

"Does it look like I have legs?" the book answered, turning around and settling back against Philip's pillows.

———~~~———

"Oh Philip, congratulations!" his mother said when he came into the kitchen. She opened the bakery box she was carrying. Inside were two giant corn muffins. "I thought you would enjoy a treat after winning the contest. Unless you're still full," she chuckled.

Philip's face fell. He looked down at his blue ribbon, which still had spatters of mud on the edges.

"Philip, what's bothering you?"

His mother's words brought it all back: the shouts from the crowd, running from Bradly, Rachel, and Ronnie, but then also the portrait of his great-great-great grandsire, and now, the Big Red Book complaining on his bed only a moment ago.

Philip wasn't sure what his mother would say when he told her about the book.

She might make him give it back.

Then I will never learn how to get rich, he thought.

"Mom," Philip started. "Are we really related to the founder of Pennyville?"

His mother looked surprised.

"Yes," she said, as she put a muffin on a plate for Philip. "He's your great-great-great-grandsire."

Philip took a bite and chewed it thoughtfully.

"He must have been really rich to build a whole town."

Philip's mother shook her head in agreement.

"Actually, when he came to Pennyville, though, all he had was a single penny."

"So that's true?"

"Yes," his mother answered. "That's how the town got its name."

"Had he always been poor?"

"No," his mother answered. "Not really. He grew up in a family of means."

"Umm, a family of what?"

His mother laughed.

"A family of 'means' is one that has enough money to do a lot of things. So, Philip the First went to the best schools and got to travel around the world with his family. He saw lots of different animals and how they lived."

"That means they were rich," Philip said, excitedly. "Did they find a treasure, or were they just all born rich?"

"Neither," his mother said. "They built wealth, just like Philip built the town of Pennyville."

"I understand how you can build a town," Philip said, remembering when all the animals came together to build a new barn and, at another time, the school's playground. "But how do you build wealth? You can't build it with boards and nails."

"You're right," his mother said, clearing away the dishes. "Philip and his family built their fortune. They learned, understood, and chose to follow *the principles of building wealth.*"

Philip didn't understand what his mother was saying. He thought that animals got rich by finding treasure or getting important jobs.

Maybe his mother was wrong.

Then he got an idea.

He would ask the book.

Chapter 3

MAY THE JOURNEY BEGIN

P hilip's thoughts whirled while he helped his mother wash the dishes: the Big Red Book had offered to teach Philip the secret of getting rich, and confirmed what Mr. Webber had said: that Philip was not the only pig who has had four slots.

Why do I have these four slots? he thought, a question he had asked himself many times.

Philip trotted back to his room. The Big Red Book's eyes were closed, and its pages fluttered as it snored.

"Big Red Book," Philip called, gently poking the cover.

"Hmmph, what?" The book opened its eyes.

"You were going to teach me the secret of getting rich," Philip said.

"Was I?"

"Yeah," Philip said. "But Mom says that my great-great-great grandsire, Philip the First, built wealth on 'principles.' I don't know what that means. Anyway, *you* said 'work ethic,' so which one of you is right?" Philip asked.

"Can't we both be right?"

"Huh?"

"What if the secret to getting rich *is* building wealth based on principles?"

"But what does that mean?" Philip asked. "I don't even know what principles are."

"Yes, you do," the book said. "You already have principles."

"I don't think so."

The book chuckled, its pages fluttering. "You talked about bullies before."

"Yeah." Philip studied the floor.

"They made fun of you, right?"

Philip nodded.

"Well," the book said. "You're bigger than they are. Why didn't you clobber them?"

"I wouldn't hit anyone!"

"All right," the book said. "Then why didn't you at least say hurtful things back?

"Because," Philip sputtered. "Because it's not right. Nobody should say mean things or try to hurt other animals. Saying or doing mean things doesn't make anything better anyway."

"Exactly!" the book said, flinging its cover wide. "You have principles!"

Philip listened, hoping to understand.

"Principles are just ideas or thoughts that help us make decisions," the book said. "They are the reasons *why* you do something, or *why* you don't."

"Mom said he built wealth on principles," Philip started. "But you said 'work ethic.'"

"That's right," the book said, with a note of triumph in its voice. "A strong work ethic is one of the most important principles for building wealth. A strong work ethic means that you do what needs to be done and take care of your responsibilities."

"You mean like cleaning my room?" Philip's heart sunk a little. "But Mom didn't *ask* me to clean it today . . ."

"Philip," the book smiled, closing its covers decisively. "You're not a baby piglet anymore. You don't need to always wait for someone to tell you what to do. When you see a job that needs to be done, you should be willing to do it. That's called self-motivation, and it's an important part of a strong work ethic."

"I should do something *even if it isn't my chore?*"

"Exactly," the book said. "And cleaning your room isn't just making your room *look* tidy. It's about paying attention to details, even in those places no one else would think to look, because you want to do a good job."

"You want me to clean those toys out from under my bed, don't you?"

"I can't *give* you a strong work ethic," the book said. "You have to choose to do it *because it's the right thing to do*. And this goes for all things."

Philip crawled under his bed and pulled out the toys. He sorted them and put each one where it belonged. Then he noticed the dust bunnies that had taken up residence there as well. He went to the kitchen to get the broom and dustpan.

"What are you doing, darling?" his mother asked as she opened mail at the table.

"Just cleaning under my bed," Philip sighed.

Her eyes opened wide in surprise, but she smiled.

After he was finished and had put the broom away, Philip looked around his room. It did seem better.

He wondered how long he could keep it like this.

"Do I have to do this all the time?" Philip asked.

The book was silent for a minute.

"I see you have a blue ribbon," it finally said.

"Yeah. I won it at the county fair's corn-eating contest."

"So you just went there and they gave it to you?"

"No," Philip laughed. "I had to compete with a lot of other animals."

"So," the book said. "You just showed up on a whim, competed, and won, correct?"

"No way," Philip said. "I practiced for weeks so I could win."

"Every day?"

"Yes, every day," Philip replied.

"If you want your work ethic to grow stronger, don't you think you should work on it every day too?" the book asked.

"Yeah," Philip said. "But how do I strengthen my work ethic?"

"By looking around you every day," the book said. "Look for the things that you can do that will make the world around you a better place. A strong work ethic is the first wealth-building principle, and one of the most important."

"Maybe it's time you should start writing your own Big Red Book," the book said.

"Really?"

"Certainly," said the book.

"Does it have to be red?" Philip asked, searching his bookshelf for a notebook.

"No, choose any color you want."

Philip found an old spiral notebook with plenty of blank pages, and it happened to be blue. He tore out the old pages and put them in the recycling bin. Then he wrote "Philip's Big Blue Book" on the cover.

On the first page he wrote:

How to Get Rich

Build wealth on principles.

Principles

1. Have a strong work ethic.

    Be self-motivated.

    Pay attention to the details.

    Strengthen your work ethic every day.

Chapter 4

TENFOLD

Over the next few days, Philip tried to keep his eyes open and see what he could do to make the world around him a better place. He noticed that the shed needed cleaning. So he cleaned it. He noticed that the front porch needed sweeping. So he swept it. He noticed that the autumn leaves needed to be raked up. So he did that too.

As he was putting the last of the leaves into the compost pile, Philip noticed something else.

Ms. Molly was raking her leaves too.

Or she was trying to, anyway.

Ms. Molly was the elderly mare who lived next door. She had raked some of the leaves that had fallen from her maple trees into a pile but then had to stop and rest. By the time she started raking again, the piled leaves had blown around the yard.

She wasn't getting very far.

Philip grabbed his rake and trotted over.

"Let me help you with that, Ms. Molly."

"Oh, thank you, Philip," she replied. "I'm just not as spry as I used to be."

"You can rest for a little while," Philip said. "I'll take care of it for you."

"That's so kind," Ms. Molly said, and she went inside.

Suddenly, Philip heard a voice.

"Four Slots!"

Philip looked up and saw Bradly, Rachel, and Ronnie walking down the hill.

"Aw, did you make that for us?" Bradly sneered, as he eyed the big pile of leaves.

"No, I—" Philip started.

"Come on!" Bradly shouted.

He and Ronnie ran and jumped into the pile Philip had so carefully raked together. Rachel fluttered her wings and cawed as the two jumped and threw leaves at each other. Philip loudly asked them to stop, but Bradly and Ronnie were not paying any attention to him.

"Looks like you're doing a crummy job," Bradly said, getting up.

Philip looked around. It looked like he had never raked at all.

The three bullies ran off, laughing.

Philip sighed and started raking all over again. It seemed to take forever, but he eventually got all the leaves collected and into the compost pile.

Ms. Molly's yard was now as neat as his own.

"Philip, how kind of you," came a voice.

He turned to see his mother trotting up the walk to Ms. Molly's home.

"He's been very helpful," Ms. Molly said, coming out onto her porch. "In fact, Philip, I want to give you this."

The mare held out a shiny penny.

"Oh, no thank you," Philip said. "I really didn't do it to get paid. I just wanted to help you."

"Well, I appreciate it," Ms. Molly said. "Look for an apple pie in the next day or so."

"And we will appreciate *that*," Philip's mother said with a smile as she and Philip turned toward home.

"Why didn't you take the penny?" Philip's mother asked as they walked to the door.

Philip thought about it.

Raking didn't seem all that difficult, and it really helped Ms. Molly. It didn't matter what the bullies had said: when he was helping Ms. Molly, he felt so happy and proud of himself. Almost as proud as when he won the blue ribbon.

"Well," Philip said, trying to find the right words. "Ms. Molly needed help. And I could give it. That's worth more than a penny. It's worth more than any kind of money."

The smile that spread across his mother's face assured him that he had found exactly the right words.

Later, when he was getting ready for bed, Philip told the Big Red Book what had happened.

"Ahhh," the book said. "You have started thinking about forms of wealth."

"'Forms of wealth'? I thought wealth and being rich just meant having a lot of money."

"You are incorrect," the book said, shaking its cover firmly. "Wealth comes in many different forms."

"Oh, I get it," Philip said. "Like you can have money, or gold bars, or diamonds—"

"No," the book interrupted, clapping its covers together. "It means the things that are important in a full life."

Philip stopped.

"Think about it," the book said. "What if you had a wonderful home full of everything you wanted but you were there all by yourself. Would you be happy?"

"My mom wouldn't be there? And friends wouldn't come over?" Philip asked.

"Nope."

"I would miss my mom," Philip said immediately. "And who would I play with?"

"Exactly," the Big Red Book said. "Family and friends are forms of wealth. They make life worth living."

"Are there other forms of *wealth*?" Philip asked. "What about being good at sports, or music, or telling jokes?"

"Yes, exactly. You understand," the book nodded. "Anything that makes life better, that makes life worth living, is a form of wealth."

Philip thought about it for a minute.

"So," he started. "When I helped Ms. Molly, I was building a form of wealth, even though I didn't take her penny?"

"You were," the book said. "You made two important steps toward building wealth. You showed a strong work ethic by offering to do extra work, and you also helped her out of the kindness of your heart. Kindness is a priceless form of wealth."

"I know it's nice, but how can kindness be wealth?"

"Because it's so strong," the book said. "In fact, whatever

26

you give from the goodness of your heart comes back to you tenfold."

"Really?" Philip asked, as he crawled under the covers.

"Wait and see," said the book, and slowly closed its pages.

Philip yawned, and before he could say another word he was sound asleep.

When Philip woke up the next morning, he thought he heard his door closing. He rubbed his eyes and sat up.

"Whoa!" he said.

Sitting on the table next to his bed was a whole stack of pennies. He picked them up and counted them.

". . . seven, eight, nine, ten," Philip counted. He jumped out of bed and ran from his room. "Mom!"

He skidded to a stop in the kitchen. His mother looked down at him with a smile.

"Mom, I found these next to my bed," Philip said, with the bright pennies spilling from his hooves.

"Yes," his mother said. "I'm so proud of you. You have been helping out around the barn, and I didn't even need to ask. You helped Ms. Molly and didn't accept a cent. I thought that you should have a reward."

"Thanks, Mom," Philip said, hugging her.

"What are you going to do with those pennies?"

"I don't know yet," Philip said.

"Maybe this will help you keep your pennies safe." His mother handed him a little jelly jar.

Philip poured his pennies into the jar. He loved the clinking sound they made in the glass. He carried his fortune back to his room and spread it out on his bed. He could think of lots of different things to do with his pennies.

"I could get a comic book, or a candy bar," Philip mumbled to himself. "Hmmm, I wonder how much a caramel apple would cost?"

"Well," the Big Red Book said, opening its covers and eyeing the pile of coins. "I see that you still have a lot to learn about building wealth."

"What's wrong with spending my pennies?" Philip asked. "I mean, Mom said it was a reward. Besides, Philip the First had to spend money, or he could never have built the town of Pennyville."

"It's not just what you spend, but *how* you spend it that matters when it comes to wealth. And I am not talking about only money," the book said.

"So, how did Philip the First spend *his* money?"

"He knew the difference between wants, needs, and desires," the book answered.

"What's the difference?"

"You'll need to figure that out," the book said with a big smile spreading across its cover.

Chapter 5

WE ALL HAVE
NEEDS

"I still haven't figured out the difference between needs, wants, and desires," Philip admitted to the Big Red Book one morning. It had been weeks, but he hadn't worked out an answer. "If you need something, don't you want it too? And isn't desiring and wanting the same thing?"

"Not really," the Big Red Book answered. "Needs, wants, and desires are very different things."

"How?"

"Let me tell you a story about my writer," the book said. "Maybe it will help you understand the difference between needs, wants, and desires."

Still in his pj's, Philip settled down to hear the story.

"When he was still a young pig," the book started, "Phil decided to go out into the world. He had already traveled a lot with his family as a piglet, and he knew that not every animal had all the comforts he had. He thought he could make a difference."

"Was he scared?" Philip asked.

"He was excited," the book said. "He was fulfilling his desires."

"That's one of the things you talked about."

"Yes, Phil had a deep desire to build something special that would help other animals build their own wealth. One penny wasn't a lot of money, but that didn't matter. He had a strong work ethic, so he knew he would be able to learn, and to create whatever he needed."

"But what did he do about a place to live, and food to eat?"

"He earned them," the book said. "When he first came to this area, there wasn't a town. There weren't even many animals living here. But he found a family of horses who needed some help."

"Needs—that's something else you talked about!"

"That's right," the book said. "The horses couldn't do all the work around their farm by themselves anymore. They needed a strong young pig with a good work ethic to help them. They paid Phil to work on their land. He spent some of the money he earned on things he needed, like food and clothes and a place to sleep. But he set money aside for other things as well."

"Like things he wanted and things he desired?" Philip asked. Then he got excited. "Like his desire to start a new town!"

"Yes," the book said. "But he had to meet his needs first."

The Big Red Book fluttered its pages until it found the passage it wanted. There, in curly script, Philip read these words:

We all need food, shelter, and water. But sometimes we need a hoof to hold, an ear to listen to our thoughts and dreams, and another heart to understand our worries. The one thing I will never need is a reason to help others.

Philip had never even thought about the things he needed. He never worried about having enough food, or where he would sleep at night. He had never thought about not having water.

"*Do* some animals worry about food, shelter, and water?" he asked in a small voice, suddenly sad at the thought.

"Yes," the book said softly.

Philip thought about it as he got dressed. He left the pennies next to his bed while he trotted to the store for his mother.

The store was chock full of good things to eat. It was late fall, so pumpkins, corn, and cranberries filled the windows and sat in crates, waiting to become part of someone's Thanksgiving dinner.

Philip finished his shopping and was on his way back home when he saw a goose landing at the crossroads ahead of him. The goose was wearing a small backpack.

"Thank you—I was getting airsick," Philip heard a voice say, though it didn't come from the goose. It came from *inside* the backpack.

"Excuse me, young pig," the goose said, completely ignoring his talking backpack. By now a large flock was settling on the grass nearby. "We've been heading south, but the wind doesn't seem to be getting any warmer. I'm not sure we're going the right way."

"Going on a vacation?" Philip asked.

"Oh no," the goose said. "As geese, we need to live where the air is warm. It's already too cold for us here. If we can't get down South soon, we might lose some of our flock."

"My name's Philip. I'm happy to help you." Philip spun around and pointed. "That way is south."

"Thanks, Philip. My name is George. I wish we could take you with us . . ." George looked a little uncomfortable. "It's my first time, and I'm worried I will get us lost again."

Philip wished he had a compass to give to George—then the geese would never get lost. Then Philip had another idea. He pointed to a nearby barn.

"Do you see that thing up on that barn?" Philip asked. "The big metal thing at the top?"

"You mean that thing with the rooster on it?"

"It's called a weathervane," Philip said.

"I've seen those on a lot of barns we have flown over," George said.

"Do you see the letters underneath?"

"You mean the E, S, W, and N?"

"Yes!" Philip said, excited. "Those stand for 'east,' 'south,' 'west,' and 'north.' If you go in the direction of the letter S, you will always be heading south."

George reached out with his wing and grasped Philip's hoof in a hearty shake.

"Thank you so much, young piglet," George said, all excitement. "Now all I have to do is circle a barn top and I'll never get lost again!"

"Hopefully," said the voice from George's pack.

"Thanks for taking the time to help my friends and me," George said, still ignoring his backpack. "I hope to see you again."

"That would be wonderful," Philip replied.

Philip trotted home. George had said that he *needed* to fly south. Was that one of the needs the Big Red Book talked about?

Philip trotted into the kitchen and gave the shopping basket to his mother. She was sitting at the kitchen table with papers spread around her.

"Thank you, Philip," she said without looking up from her work. "Did you get the receipt?"

"Right here, Mom," he said, pulling a paper slip from his pocket.

His mother took it and laid it on a pile of similar receipts.

"What are you doing?" Philip asked.

His mother sighed and looked up. "I'm working on our budget, Philip. I do this every month to keep track of how much we spend and how we spend it."

Philip knew that his mother sat down to work like this at the beginning of every month, but he had never thought much about it. He pulled out a chair and sat on it. His mother pushed a sheet of paper his way. It had a long list of numbers.

"This is how much I make every month," his mother explained.

"Wow! That's a lot of money."

His mother chuckled.

"It sure seems that way, but it goes pretty fast. In this column are all the things we need. These are things that we *have* to spend money on every month."

"What's that number?" Philip asked.

"That's what I pay in taxes," she replied.

"Taxes?"

"That's money that I pay to the community."

"Why?"

"It's my duty to pay taxes. It's everyone's duty," she said. "It's how we pay for the things we all share."

"Like what?"

"Like your school, for one thing," she said with a smile. "And taxes pay for roads, police, and firefighters . . ."

"You pay the fire department? But we've never had a fire."

"But they're available to us if we ever need them," she explained. "Do you remember last summer when the Lumber Mill burned down?"

Philip remembered. It was awful. The sky was all lit up over the west side of Pennyville. Animals were running everywhere. Some were escaping the fire, others were trying to put it out. No one was hurt, but Philip heard that several families near the mill lost their homes.

"The fire department worked hard to save the mill and a lot of homes that day. Some they were able to save, but some they weren't," she said. "So, none of those homeowners had to pay the fire department that night. Our taxes cover things like the fire department so they will always be here when we need them."

"I get it," Philip said.

He looked at the rest of the list. It had things like food, wood, hay. When he added it up, it was more than half of what his mother made every month. Then he looked at the list and saw a word he had never seen before.

"What's that?"

"That's the mortgage," his mother explained. "I didn't have enough money to buy our home all at once. So, I borrowed money from the bank to buy our barn, and I pay off a little of that debt every month until it's gone. That's called a mortgage."

"That's awfully nice of the bank," Philip said.

"It is," she replied. "But the bank makes money too. I have to pay back more money than I borrowed. The extra money I pay is called 'interest.'"

"That's not fair," Philip said.

"But, Philip, how else would the bank pay its employees, or build its buildings, or pay interest on savings accounts? I knew how much interest I would have to pay before I borrowed the money, and I chose to borrow it."

"I guess so," Philip said. But he noticed something interesting in what she had said. "You said that the bank pays interest as well as charges interest. Do *you* get paid interest?"

Philip's mother smiled. "I get a little bit. But I do something else to get interest, and it is one of the most important parts of my budget. It's one of the most important needs of our household."

Chapter 6

PAY YOURSELF
FIRST

Philip leaned in close, ready to hear what his mother had to say.

"Have you ever noticed Mr. Bryson coming here to the barn?"

Philip thought about it. Bryson the Bull had come around once a month for as long as he could remember. He nodded.

"That's because every month when I get paid, the first thing I do is put aside a portion of the money I have earned, and I invest it," she said. "This is called paying myself first."

"But I thought you gave the money to Mr. Bryson."

His mother laughed.

"Mr. Bryson is my investor. He invests the money in a lot of different ways so that I always have money that is growing. It's working all the time."

"Even on the weekends?" Philip asked.

"Even when I'm sleeping," she answered.

"How does it do that?"

"It's called compound interest," she said.

"It pounds on something?"

His mother laughed.

"No, *com*pound interest."

"But isn't it hard to pay yourself before you get to buy anything?"

"Yes, it is," she said. "But that's why I exercise financial discipline. It's one of the principles I follow."

Another principle! Philip couldn't wait to ask the Big Red Book about it.

"Thanks, Mom." Philip jumped up and headed back to his bedroom. The book was on his bed, lying open in a beam of sunshine.

"What do you know about . . ." Philip blurted, then paused for just a moment to remember the words his mother had used. "Compound interest?"

"Oh, compound interest?" The book said, pages beginning to tremble. "Nothing much. Just that IT'S ONE OF THE MOST POWERFUL WEALTH BUILDERS ON EARTH!"

The Big Red Book's pages fluttered wildly, then stopped. Suddenly casual, it said, "Other than that, I know nothing."

Philip giggled. So did the Big Red Book.

"What makes it so powerful?" he asked.

"It's pretty simple," the book explained. "Imagine you put one hundred pennies in an account that pays compound interest. Let's pretend the account pays ten pennies a year for every hundred pennies in it. That would be ten percent."

"Okay."

"So how many pennies would you have after a year?"

"One hundred and ten pennies," Philip said, working it out in his head.

"And how many would you have after two years?"

"One hundred and twenty pennies," Philip said. "I don't understand the big—"

"WRONG!" the book exclaimed. You would have one hundred and twenty-one pennies."

"But you said ten pennies per one hundred, right?"

"Yes, but the second year, you would be starting with one hundred and ten pennies. Those extra ten pennies would earn interest too. The second year, you would earn an extra penny more than you did the first year."

"Then, would I earn two extra pennies the next year?" Philip asked.

"You got it!" The book said. "Compound interest means that the interest you have earned also earns its own interest, making even more money for you. So, you earn a little more every year, even if you don't add any money to your account."

"Wow, that's cool."

"Oh, it's more than cool," the book said. "It means that you could literally turn one dollar into a million dollars if you lived long enough."

"Then I would be rich!" Philip looked over at the pennies on his nightstand.

"No, then you would have a million dollars," the book corrected. "It's what you do with that million dollars that makes you rich or not."

"Is that what Mom meant by the principle of financial discipline?"

"That is an important principle," the book said. "My writer

thought that financial discipline was almost as important as a strong work ethic."

"Isn't it more important to earn money?"

"Well, it's just as important to understand what to do with the money you have earned." The book opened its pages to show a picture of a strong young boar in a pair of patched overalls working in a field.

"Phil worked hard. He spent money on the things he needed, but he took care of what he had so that he could save money too. If he could patch his overalls, he did it instead of buying a new pair."

The book turned its page to a photograph of Phil walking through a county fair much like the one Philip had just attended. All around him, animals were carrying stuffed toys, cotton candy, and balloons, but Phil's hands were empty.

He was smiling.

"Phil liked to go out and spend time with other animals. He liked to have fun. He was just very careful with the money he earned."

The book flipped another page, and now Philip was looking at Phil standing in front of a large empty field. He was smiling and handing some money to a horse.

"He saved his money until he could purchase a small field. But he kept working for the horses while he tended his own fields. This meant he could earn even more money."

"Like compound interest," Philip said, putting it together.

"Yes, kind of like compound interest," the book agreed. "Only he wasn't investing in a bank. He was investing in himself."

Philip thought about that for a minute. Then he reached over and pulled out his blue spiral notebook to add some important words.

How to Get Rich

Build wealth on principles.

Principles

1. Have a strong work ethic.
   Be self-motivated.
   Pay attention to the details.
   Strengthen your work ethic every day.

2. Understand needs, wants, and desires.
   Needs: food, shelter, water, and investing in yourself.

3. Use financial discipline.
   Compound interest is one of the most powerful wealth-building tools on Earth.

Chapter 7

WE ALL HAVE
WANTS

T he season turned cold, and every animal in Pennyville was busy preparing for the winter holidays. Philip's ten pennies stayed in the jar on the shelf. He was wondering if buying presents was a need or something else.

"I understand what you mean when you talk about needs," he said to the Big Red Book, which was resting on his nightstand. He was thinking of his mother's budget and George's trip south. "But what about wants?"

The Big Red Book flipped through several of its pages and then stopped. Philip looked closely at the smooth, flowing script he had seen before...

———❧———

In my life, there will be many things of which my heart grows fond. Some will be of true value, and other things will not.

If I am not happy with what I have, I will never be content with what I want.

While pursuing my wants, I will always consider the needs of others.

It is only when my list of wants mirrors my list of needs that I will know I have everything of true value.

I understand that the best way to earn what I want in life is to learn what others want and to help them get it.

———❧———

Philip read the words carefully. Twice.

"Does that mean that Philip the First never wanted a toy or a game for himself? That he never bought presents for anyone else?"

"Not at all," the book said, closing thoughtfully. "There were many things that he saw and wanted, for a while."

The book paused, then continued. "Have you ever wanted something so badly that you knew you had to have it? But once you got it, you were disappointed?"

Philip thought for a minute. He remembered a game that he had seen at the store. Every young animal playing was cheering and having a wonderful time. He knew that, if he got that game, everyone would want to come to play at his home. Finally, his mother gave him the game for his birthday. He couldn't wait to play it with friends. However, he found it to be so boring that he got tired of it after a day.

"Yeah," Philip answered. "I think so."

"What Phil meant was that, if you aren't happy with what you have, you won't be happy with what you get. That's why he always had an attitude of gratitude."

"I like that," Philip said. "It rhymes. Does that mean he was always grateful?"

"He surely tried to be," the book said. "But it goes a little deeper than that. It meant that he *looked for* things to be grateful for. You will always find what you're looking for. If you're looking for things to complain about, you'll find that too."

"So, if I look for what I want, I'll find that too?"

"You know it," the book said.

"Phil-iip . . . ," his mother called. "I'm going downtown. Would you like to come with me?"

"Coming, Mom," Philip said, and slid off his bed.

"Think about it," said the Big Red Book. "And why don't you ask your mom what she has for wants?"

Philip thought about all this as he trotted down the road beside his mother.

"Mom," he finally said. "You have a whole list of things that we need in our budget, but what about spending money on things you want?"

"I do that too," she replied.

"What kind of things do you spend that money on?"

"Well," she said. "Sometimes I spend it on things like corn muffins for a first-place piglet."

Philip smiled. "Those were good. But what about other months?"

"There's something I do every month that I *really* want."

"And what is that?"

"I pay a little extra toward our debts."

"Huh?"

"The bank requires me to pay them a certain amount every month, to eventually pay off what we borrowed for the barn, plus interest. Every month I pay the bank a little more than they require."

"Is that okay with the bank?"

"Of course. And this way we will own the barn a little faster *and* pay a little less interest."

"Why is that a 'want'?"

"Think about it," his mother said. "When I am done paying the mortgage, I will be able to split up my money differently. I will have more money to spend on my desires and on helping others."

Philip thought about it as they walked. He had seen the budget list and how much money his mother spent every month on the mortgage. If she didn't have to pay that anymore, she would have a *lot* more money.

By the time they got to the village, Philip was deep in thought. What did *he* really want?

While his mother went into the bank, Philip stayed outside looking through the window of the General Store. In one corner of the window display, there was a tree covered with toys, books, and glitter. A train chugged around the bottom. Stuffed animals, blocks, and games were all around.

In the other corner was a giant toy box with a sign that read TOY DRIVE. The box was already full to the brim with toys. At the top there was a toy race car as well as a Cathy Caterpillar doll.

"Does itty-bitty Four Slots want a teddy bear?"

Philip spun around and saw Bradly, Ronnie, and Rachel staring back at him.

"Leave me alone, Bradly," Philip said, feeling the window against his back.

"Aw, you scared?" Bradly laughed. Rachel and Ronnie echoed him.

"I mean it," Philip said. "My mom's right inside the bank, and everyone can see you."

Looking around at all the shoppers out and about, Bradly stepped back.

"You go tell your mommy," Bradly said.

Philip walked away.

49

"Philip!"

Philip looked around and saw Mr. Webber putting up the wreaths on the door of the Town Hall.

"Could you hand me that bow?"

Philip trotted over to grab a bow that had blown down the sidewalk and brought it back to the old turtle.

"These will brighten up the old Town Hall," Mr. Webber said.

Philip turned around to see that Bradly and his gang were already gone. He looked up and down the street.

Then he saw them. They were inside the toy store.

Rachel fluttered to the tree in the window and looked around. Then, as Philip watched, Bradly snatched the Cathy Caterpillar doll from the top of the toy pile.

"Did you see that?" Philip said.

"What?" Mr. Webber said, turning around.

But Bradly had disappeared from the window.

Would Mr. Webber believe me? Philip wondered.

"Nothing," Philip mumbled.

"Thank you," Mr. Webber said. "You're a piglet I can count on."

"Thank you, sir," Philip said with pride in his chest. But he felt his spirits deflate when he saw the trio emerge. Bradly had a bulge under his shirt.

Philip couldn't believe it. Bradly had stolen from the toy drive! He had stolen from someone who might not get a Christmas toy now.

Philip was about to say something to Mr. Webber as he watched the bullies run down the road, laughing the entire way.

Philip knew what he wanted.

He wanted to get those bullies off his back. He wanted them to leave him alone.

Chapter 8

WE ALL HAVE
DESIRES

F inally, the frenzy of Christmas was over, and little animals everywhere were getting back into the routine of home and school.

Philip had written his thank-you notes a little differently this year. He really tried to show how much he appreciated each of the neighbors who had come by with a gift or a treat. He wanted to keep that "attitude of gratitude" all year round.

But there were plenty of things that Philip was still struggling to learn.

"I understand the differences between what I want and what I need," Philip told the Big Red Book one morning as he was getting ready for school. "But what about desires? How are desires different from things I want?"

The Big Red Book flipped through its pages and opened to another passage by Philip the First:

———〜〜〜———

Desire is born in the heart and is the starting point for many great achievements. I will work hard and smart, be fair and considerate of others, and my greatest desires will become my reality. I will learn about what others desire and help them get it. It is then when my own desires are fulfilled.

———〜〜〜———

"Do you understand?"

"I think so," Philip said. "I think it is saying I have to listen to my heart and the hearts of those around me."

"That's part of it," the book said. "But it also means that you have to figure out the 'why' of your dreams."

"Huh?"

"Think about it," the book said. "What if you wanted to go on a trip. Is it a want or a desire?"

"How can I tell?"

"You have to look in your heart and find out *why* you want to go and what you want it to do for you. If you want to go on a trip because it looks like fun, or because all your friends are going, it might be a 'want.'"

"So, I shouldn't go," Philip said.

"Not necessarily," the book said quickly. "It's important to do some things you want. Everyone needs a little fun."

"But," the book continued. "What if there was a deeper reason?"

"To go on a trip?"

"Sure," the book said. "What if you wanted to go to help animals in another part of the world? What if you wanted to go someplace to learn how other animals lived, or to find out how they did something new that would make life better here? Those are deeper reasons and show that you might have a desire to go instead of just a want."

"Because the trip might help me achieve a dream," Philip said.

"Exactly," the book said.

Philip thought back to the very first day he had opened the book. He had wanted to get rich. That was a desire, wasn't it?

Philip's face got hot. He realized that simply having money wasn't a dream. It wasn't a desire.

It was only about himself.

What about other animals? What about his mother? What about his friends?

"Does everyone have desires?" Philip said.

"We all have desires," the book said, drumming his pages thoughtfully. "Without a desire to change, nothing really happens in the world. Nothing changes. It's our desires that shape our choices, and our choices shape our lives."

Philip wondered about what other animals might desire. He wondered what it was *he* really desired in his own life.

He had a lot to add to his own blue book.

How to Get Rich

Build wealth on principles.

Principles

1. Have a strong work ethic.
   Be self-motivated.
   Pay attention to the details.
   Strengthen your work ethic every day.

2. Understand needs, wants, and desires.

   Needs: food, shelter, water, and investing in yourself.

   Wants: things that will make you happy.

   Desires: help you achieve your dreams and the dreams of others.

3. Use financial discipline.

   Compound interest is one of the most powerful wealth-building tools on Earth.

   Keep an attitude of gratitude.

   Paying off debts early leaves you more money for other things later.

56

Just then, Philip's door opened.

"Oh, you're up and dressed. I'm glad to see it," his mother said. "I have good news for you: it's a snow day!"

Philip whooped for joy and ran to his window, all thoughts of the Philip the First flying from his mind. Everywhere he looked, all he saw was deep, crisp snow.

His mother made him a warm breakfast of cheese grits.

"Mom," Philip asked. "What is your deepest desire?"

"My what?" his mother laughed.

"What do you desire more than anything else?"

She thought for a minute.

"I guess, I really just want you to grow up happy and healthy and wise."

Wow! Philip thought. *Mom's biggest desires are all things for me.*

Philip's mother made him bundle up warm before she let him go outside to play in the snow. He broke through the snow drifts around the shed, and in a flash he found his silver snow sled.

It may not have looked like much, but he loved it. He had made it from an old trashcan lid that had lost its handle. He had banged out the dents with a hammer and cleaned it with a scouring pad. For the finishing touch he had added three coats of beeswax to the bottom so that it would go extra fast.

Philip dragged the sled through the deep snow to the big sledding hill behind Ms. Molly's orchard. Half the young animals in Pennyville had already gathered on the hill. There were wooden sleds with metal runners and also other trashcan lids like Philip's. Some animals were simply doing belly flops and sliding down the hill on their stomachs.

Everyone was laughing and having a wonderful time.

Until Bradly showed up.

"Give me that," Bradly said to Lily.

"B-but I just got it for Christmas," the little llama said.

"Great! So it's new."

Bradly threw himself on the brand-new sled and flew down the hill like a runaway freight train. He slammed into Dickey and Mickey the chicken twins before he finally slowed at the bottom.

"Are you all right?" Philip asked, as he pulled the chicks out of a snowbank.

"I'm f-f-f-fine," said Dickey, obviously shaken.

"M-m-me too," said Mickey.

Philip turned to Bradly, who was pulling the sled back up the hill for another run.

"You could have really hurt them," Philip said.

"So what?" Bradly said. "They need to be tougher."

"That's not your sled, either."

"It is now," Bradly said.

At the top of the hill, Lily was crying.

Philip squared his shoulders.

"No. It's. Not."

Bradly laughed. "What are you going to do about it, Four Slots? Tell your mama? Little baby."

"No," Philip said, leaning closer and using a softer voice.

"I'm going to tell Mr. Webber about who took the doll from the toy drive."

Philip looked Bradly squarely in the eye when he said it.

For just a second, Philip thought he saw fear in Bradly's eyes. But the look disappeared so fast Philip wondered if he had imagined it.

"Don't even think about it, Four Slots," Bradly said. "Or I will pound you into the dust."

Then he shoved Philip.

Philip rolled, tail over snout, all the way down the hill until he reached the bottom, sore and cold. Before he could even stand up, he felt something hit him in the head.

It was his own sled, bent in half.

Philip sniffled as he dragged his sled home. He thought about his deepest desire. It wasn't just for him. It was for all the young animals in Pennyville.

I want those bullies to be nice!

Chapter 9

DO THE RIGHT THING

It seemed to Philip that it would never stop snowing. He had been able to bend his sled back into shape, although he didn't think it went as fast as it used to. Every time he went to the sledding hill, he kept one eye open for Bradly, Rachel, and Ronnie.

Arriving home after school one day, Philip was thinking how tired he was of running from them. And he was tired of being "Four Slots" every day at school.

Philip dragged his backpack into his room. He began to pull out his books and notebooks. Then he saw his red book lying on his desk. He suddenly pushed it onto the floor, then dropped his head into his hooves.

"What's up, Buttercup?" the Big Red Book asked. "You certainly don't look cheerful."

"I thought you were going to teach me what my four slots are for," Philip said, closer to tears than he wanted to be. "But you haven't done anything. I just wish I was like every other animal."

"No, you don't," the book said. "You're different because it takes different animals to make a difference in the world. You're going to make that difference, Philip. You just have to give yourself a chance."

"I don't know if I believe you anymore," Philip said.

"Phil-iip," Philip's mother called.

Philip sighed and headed to the kitchen, where he saw his mother at the table, which was again covered with papers. *Oh yeah*, thought Philip, *it's the beginning of the month again.*

"Oh, Philip," she said. "I'm so sorry to ask you, but I'm swamped at the moment. Could you please deliver this envelope to Mr. Bryson for me?"

"Sure, Mom," Philip said with a sigh.

"I'll have your favorite dinner ready when you get back. How does that sound?"

"Sounds good," Philip said in a low voice.

He put on his hat and scarf against the winter chill and headed out into the fading daylight. Philip trotted down the road, but he felt too discouraged to hold his head up. Instead, he kept his eyes on the path in front of him all the way into town.

"Whoa there!"

Philip looked up and saw that he had almost walked into Mr. Webber. The old turtle was pushing a snow shovel up the walkway to the City Hall.

"I'm sorry," Philip said. "Isn't it late to be shoveling the walk?"

"I want to clear the snow before it freezes overnight," Mr. Webber said.

Philip could see the turtle shivering in his shell.

"Why don't you let me finish," he offered. "It will just take a moment."

"Thank you," Mr. Webber said, stamping his feet. "I will have some cocoa ready inside when you're done."

"Thank you," Philip said. "But I have to deliver something for my mother."

"All right," Mr. Webber said with a twinkle in his eye. "Another time then. Just leave the shovel next to the door."

Philip took the shovel from Mr. Webber and started scraping it across the walkway. It was just a few minutes before he was scraping away the last line of snow. Then he noticed that quite a bit of snow had piled up in front of Mr. Bryson's office. He already had the shovel, and it would be easier to walk up a cleared sidewalk anyway, so Philip pushed the shovel back and forth, plowing the layer of snow to the side of the walk. As he was finishing, he noticed that he had uncovered something. He saw the corner of a piece of paper sticking up, almost invisible against the snow. He reached down and pulled, and suddenly he was holding a thick envelope. There was no name on the envelope, so Philip opened it to find out who it belonged to. There wasn't a name inside the envelope either.

Instead, there were ten one-dollar bills.

"Ten dollars!" Philip said aloud. He could hardly believe his good luck!

Finders keepers, losers weepers! he thought.

He heard this all the time at school.

But this time he wasn't the loser!

Philip thought about one of the times he had lost something. He had received a shiny silver dollar for his birthday, and he wanted to show everyone at school. However, little did he know that he had a hole in his pocket, and he lost it on the walk to school that day. He never did find that coin.

I wonder who lost this money? I can imagine exactly how they must feel!

Then Philip remembered who it was that always chanted, "Finders keepers, losers weepers."

It was Bradly.

"Do I really want to be like *Bradly?*" Philip asked himself aloud as he trotted up the walk. Then he wondered, *What should I do instead?*

The lights were on, and through the window Philip could see Mr. Bryson working on his ledgers. Even though most of the offices and shops in the village had closed, Mr. Bryson was still working to help animals like his mother to realize their financial desires, to help them live out their dreams.

Philip opened the door, and a little bell rang.

Mr. Bryson looked up and smiled.

"Philip," he said. "So nice to see you. Are you bringing your mother's investment?"

"Yes, sir," Philip said as he shoved his hand into his pocket. In addition to his mother's money, he knew what he needed to do with the other envelope.

"But I have something else too," he said, pulling out the envelope he had found. "I found this in the snow in front of your office. It doesn't have a name on it."

Mr. Bryson took the envelope and looked at the bills.

"Hmmm," he said. "It's dry, so it hasn't been there long. I did give a client an envelope of money today. I will check and see if he lost it."

Philip's heart sank just a little. There was a part of him that was hoping Mr. Bryson would tell him to keep it.

"I appreciate your honesty," Mr. Bryson said. "There are a lot of animals who would just keep this much money and not tell anyone.

"I couldn't do that, sir," Philip said.

Even though I wanted to, he thought.

Mr. Bryson smiled.

"I know," he said. "That's just one of the things that makes you so unique. You're going to go far in this life, my friend."

"Why do you say that?"

Mr. Bryson tapped the envelope in his hand.

"When animals know that they can trust you, you have a treasure that can never be taken from you. Trust is a magnificent form of wealth."

"Thank you, sir," Philip said, feeling proud of himself for his good deed.

He wondered if Mr. Bryson knew how hard it had been to give that money back. He thought about it the whole way home.

It was dark by the time he saw his barn ahead of him.

"There's my honest piglet," his mother said when he opened the door.

"Huh?"

"Mr. Bryson called and told me what you did," his mother said. "I'm so proud of you. That was a very honest and caring thing to do."

She put down a plate of his very favorite dinner: fresh corn dripping in butter.

Philip stayed where he was, twisting his hat in his hands.

"What's wrong?" she asked.

"Well," Philip said. "Maybe I'm not that caring."

He told his mother how much he was tempted to keep the money and how hard it was to give it away.

"Did you think doing the right thing is supposed to be easy?" she asked.

"Isn't it?"

"Absolutely not," she said with a smile. "Do you know how hard it is to pay myself first every month? Or to pay off my debts early? There are times when I would much rather spend that money on something else."

"But you do it because of financial discipline," Philip said. "That's what you told me."

"That's right," she said. "Financial discipline is necessary for building wealth. But so are other kinds of discipline. You have shown me one of your own kinds of discipline by keeping your room neat and clean. You just showed me another kind of discipline by giving back the money you found."

"Mr. Bryson was still working, even though everyone else had gone home," Philip said. "Is that a kind of discipline?"

"It sure is," she replied. "The habits you create around work ethic, honesty, and your finances are the boards that build wealth. Consistency is the nails. Does this make sense, Philip?"

Philip nodded, sat and ate his corn, then went to his room to write in his notebook:

The habits you create around things such as work ethic, honesty, and finances are the boards that build wealth. Consistency is the nails.

As Philip looked over his other entries, something caught his eye:

2. Understand needs, wants, and desires.

    Needs: food, shelter, water, and investing in yourself.

    Wants: things that will make you happy.

    Desires: help you achieve your dreams and the dreams of others.

"Hey," Philip said to the Big Red Book. "Needs, wants, and desires are three different places to put money. Does that have anything to do with my slots?"

"Finally!" the book said, clapping its covers together. "I wondered when you would put it all together."

"But I have four slots, not three," Philip said. "What's the last slot for?"

"You'll have to figure that out too," said the Big Red Book.

Chapter 10

THE FOURTH SLOT

Philip wondered and wondered what he was supposed to do with his fourth slot.

He thought about it for weeks.

But he couldn't figure it out.

"Can't you give me a hint?" he asked the Big Red Book. "What did Phil do with *his* fourth slot?"

The Big Red Book closed its covers quickly, blinked, then opened up just a little.

"What do you already know about Philip the First?"

"I know that he built Pennyville," Philip said.

"But what did he do with it?" asked the book.

"I'm not sure," Philip answered.

"Maybe if you found out, you would have a clue about the fourth slot," the Big Red Book said, closing its cover completely.

"Philip!" his mother called. "We need to get going."

"Coming, Mom," Philip said.

Philip and his mother walked down the road on one of the first warm Saturdays of spring.

"Mom," Philip asked. "What did Philip the First do after he built Pennyville?"

"Well," his mother started. "It took him a long time to build Pennyville. Then, toward the end of his life, he decided to give the town to everyone who lived here."

"He gave away an entire town?"

"Yes, he did," she replied. "He thought that everyone would benefit from his gift. He thought that the real measure of your wealth is what you do to help others."

"But why?"

"Because he knew that not everyone had the blessings he did."

While walking and chatting, Philip and his mother saw a friendly face walking their way.

"Hello, Mrs. Anthropist," came their neighbor's sweet voice.

"Well hello, Molly. It's a pleasant surprise to see you."

"Hello, Ms. Molly," Philip chimed in.

"I have some apple seedlings that are looking for a home— would you like some?" asked Ms. Molly.

"That would be delightful," Philip's mother said.

"Perfect," Ms. Molly said. "Philip, you can choose some from my greenhouse whenever you'd like."

"Thank you," Philip replied.

"I'll see you later then," Ms. Molly said, then continued on her way.

"Where do you think we should plant the seedlings, Mom?" Philip asked as they approached the grocery store.

While they gathered all their groceries Philip and his mother talked about different places they could plant the apple seedlings. They had come up with several good options by the time they got to the checkout line. Here, they were waiting behind a large badger carrying his small daughter.

"What a cute little one," Philip's mother said.

The baby badger giggled and threw her doll at Philip. He picked it up and looked at it.

It was a Cathy Caterpillar doll.

He handed it back to the baby.

"Thanks," said her father. "She loves that doll. She won't go anywhere without it."

The cashier started ringing up the man's groceries.

"Philip went through that phase when he was little," Philip's mother said, laughing.

Philip blushed to think how he still had his bright purple stuffed dinosaur in the back of his closet.

"That will be eighteen dollars," the cashier said.

The badger pulled some money from his pocket and then got a funny look on his face.

"I'm sorry," he said. "I'm going to have to put some things back." He started sorting through his bagged items.

"That won't be necessary," said Philip's mother as she pulled out her own money. She started to give some bills to the cashier, saying, "Please take this to pay for the rest."

"I can't let you—," the badger began.

"Of course you can," Philip's mother said. "You work at the Lumber Mill, don't you?"

"I *did*," he said. "It's been hard since the fire. But we're rebuilding."

"It's coming along well," she replied in agreement. "I know that once you get the mill back up and running, you'll be fine. I know how many animals your mill has helped."

"Thank you, ma'am," he said. "We always tried to help where we could."

"And now it's my turn to help," she said, handing the cashier the money.

"Thank you," he said. "I will always remember this."

Philip watched the badger leave with his daughter and groceries. While his mother paid for their own food, he saw the stranger greet a young badger outside and then walk away together.

It was Bradly.

That was Bradly's *Dad? But he seemed so kind.*

"Philip," his mother said as they began to walk home. "I want to talk to you about what happened back there."

"You paid for their groceries," Philip said. "How come?"

"Because they needed them," she replied. "Not everyone has what they need. The Badger family has had a hard time since the mill burned down. They have been working on rebuilding it, but that takes time. They had some savings, but it probably wasn't enough."

"That's not your fault."

"No, it's not," she agreed. "But it's important, to me anyway, to make sure that I put aside a little every week so that I can give back to my community, or to those who need it."

"Just like Philip the First!" Philip said. Suddenly, he told his mother he'd meet her at home, then he took off, running the rest of the way.

He burst into his room.

"'Giving back' is the fourth slot isn't it?" Philip shouted to the Big Red Book.

"What did you say?" the Big Red Book asked casually, but Philip could see the wide smile on its cover.

"The four slots are for needs, wants, desires, and giving to my community," Philip said. "I should put money in the fourth slot to give to others, right?"

"You got it!" the book shouted, opening its covers wide and fluttering the pages in celebration.

"*I got it*," Philip whispered.

"Money is one way to give," the book said. "But there are other ways as well. Can you think of them?"

Philip thought about it for a minute.

"When I helped Ms. Molly rake her leaves. That was giving too, wasn't it?"

"Yes," the Big Red Book said. "And there is another way you have experienced giving."

Philip thought and thought.

"I give up," he finally said. "Can you tell me?"

"We're doing it right now," the book said.

"You mean asking questions and finding answers?" Philip said. "How is this giving back?"

"You give back when you *share* what you've learned, when you share wisdom and knowledge."

"How so?" Philip asked.

"When you share what you have learned through your education or your own experiences, you become a mentor," the book explained. "Mentorship is one of the best ways to give to someone in need. Rather than helping an animal just for a moment, mentors give animals knowledge so they can benefit for a lifetime."

"Because knowledge is another form of wealth," Philip said, now really understanding.

"By George, I think you've got it!" the book pronounced, bouncing on the bed.

The book paused for a moment to let Philip take it all in.

"But the next question is," it finally continued, "how many pennies are you going to put in each slot?"

The book settled into a comfortable spot on the bed and slowly closed, leaving Philip alone with his thoughts.

Philip couldn't think of an answer right away, but he knew he needed to write down what he had learned. So, he started there.

How to ~~Get Rich~~ Build Wealth

Build wealth on principles.

Principles

1. Have a strong work ethic.

  Be self-motivated.
  Pay attention to the details.
  Strengthen your work ethic every day.

The habits you create around things such as work ethic, honesty, and finances are the boards that build wealth. Consistency is the nails.

2. Understand needs, wants, and desires.

Needs: food, shelter, water, and investing in yourself.

Wants: things that will make you happy.

Desires: help you achieve your dreams and the dreams of others.

Giving wealth to others: time, money, knowledge and mentorship, a helping hoof, a listening ear, and a compassionate heart.

3. Use financial discipline.

Compound interest is one of the most powerful wealth-building tools on Earth.

Keep an attitude of gratitude.

Paying off debts early leaves you more money for other things later.

4. With my differences, I can make a difference in the world.

5. Doing what is right is not always easy.

6. My slots have to do with needs, wants, desires, and the needs of others.

7. There are many forms of wealth. Knowledge and trust are two great forms.

Happiness is my #1.

Chapter 11

THE LAST THREE PENNIES

Philip went to his shelf and opened the jelly jar of pennies.

He held them in his hooves, watching the light glint off their shiny copper surface.

"So," the Big Red Book said from its perch on the shelf, riffling its pages thoughtfully. "How are you going to use your four slots?"

Philip smiled.

"First, I need to figure out which slot to use for each principle. What did Philip the First do?"

"Don't ask me," the book said. "There are some things you need to figure out for yourself."

"Hmmm," Philip said. "I think I will use the first slot for my needs."

"Why your first slot?"

"Well, I don't really have any needs right now, but using the first slot will remind me to pay myself first. So, he put a penny in his first slot.

"Sounds like that will cultivate good habits," the book said.

"And I think I will use my fourth slot for helping others," Philip said. And he put two pennies in that slot.

"That's a generous choice," the book said.

"I'm not really sure about my desires right now," Philip said.

"But I have some ideas. I want to be ready when I know for sure."

Philip had a satisfying feeling as he dropped a penny in his third slot.

"And there are always things that I want," Philip said. But right now what I *want* is to make sure that I'm investing that money the best possible way, so . . ."

One penny went into his second slot.

"What are you going to do with the rest?" the book asked.

Philip only smiled and didn't give the book an answer.

That night, Philip went to sleep feeling full of hope.

The next morning, Philip put the other five pennies in his pocket and took the empty jar to his mother.

"You can have this back now, Mom."

"You don't need it anymore?"

"Not any more," Philip said. "I figured out what to do with my pennies."

"Can you tell me what you decided?" she asked.

"Well, I thought about everything you told me about Philip the First."

And everything I learned from the Big Red Book, he thought.

"You said you pay for your needs first, including paying yourself. You take care of all my needs, so I don't have to pay for those yet. But I still paid myself ten percent just like you do. So, I put a penny in one of my slots for my future needs."

"Good idea, little piglet."

"Then I put in a penny each for both my wants and desires. I haven't made a plan for either of those yet, but I want to be ready."

"Another good idea," his mother replied.

"Then I put two pennies in my slot to help others. That way I'll be ready if someone needs help."

"That's a very kind plan," she said, taking his hooves into her own. "I'm very proud of you, Philip."

"But," she added, "that's only five pennies. What are you going to do with the other five?"

"I have an idea," Philip said. "Can I tell you tonight?"

"Of course, Philip. After all, it's your money."

Philip smiled, glad that his mother trusted him. He just hoped he was making the right decision.

Philip left the house and walked down the path. He knew where he was going, but he almost hoped he was wrong about who would be there.

"Beautiful day, isn't it?"

Philip turned and saw Mr. Webber sitting on the bench in front of the Town Hall, basking in the sun. "Kind of makes you wish it was really spring."

"Yes, sir," Philip said, swallowing the lump in his throat.

"And where are you off to?" Mr. Webber asked, raising his eyebrows.

"Umm," Philip started. "I'm . . ."

Philip wasn't sure how to explain what he was doing or why he was doing it.

"Run along and have fun with your friends, Philip," Mr. Webber said, his eyes twinkling. "I have a feeling you're off to do great things."

Philip gulped, then nodded. He walked past the school,

empty on the weekend, and past the movie theater filled with matinee viewers. He carefully walked onto the empty lot behind the theater. There was an old popcorn machine there, and several rows of older movie seats thrown every which way.

But, just as he expected, one row of seats sat upright under a tree. Bradly was sprawled over two of the seats while Rachel was perched on the arm of a seat nearby. Ronnie was trying to do a cartwheel while the other two laughed.

Philip swallowed.

Then suddenly Bradly turned, and Philip was looking him straight in the eye.

"What are you doing here, Four Slots?" Bradly asked, jumping from his seat.

"I have something for you," Philip said with as much bravery as he could muster. "For each of you actually."

Rachel flew over and perched on an old crate.

"What have you got for me?" she said, cocking her head to one side.

Philip held out a penny.

"Oooh! Shiny!" Rachel proclaimed as she snatched it out of Philip's hoof.

"Me too?" Ronnie asked, getting up and running over.

"Here you go," Philip said, dropping another penny into his paw.

"I'm getting some candy," Ronnie said, already running toward town.

"Wait for me," Rachel cawed as she followed.

Philip and Bradly were left alone in the empty lot.

"If you think I want your stupid penny—," Bradly started.

"I'm not sure what you want," Philip said, and realized it was true. He had never really talked to Bradly.

"What," Bradly said, cracking his knuckles. "Do you think if you give me a penny, I won't beat you up?"

"I can't make you do anything," Philip said. "But I hope you don't want to hurt anyone, including me."

"For one stupid penny," Bradly said. "You can't do anything with a penny."

"Our town was founded with only one penny," Philip said softly.

"It was not," Bradly replied in disbelief.

"Yes, it was. Philip the First only had a penny when he came here."

Bradly's face changed. He didn't look mad exactly. He didn't even look mean.

Philip thought he looked curious.

"But, why would *you* give me anything?" Bradly asked.

"Because whatever you do out of the kindness of your heart will come back to you tenfold," Philip explained.

"Does not," Bradly said.

"It surely does," Philip replied. "That's how I got these pennies."

"I get it," Bradly laughed. Now he sounded like the old, mean Bradly again. "So, you think that if you give *me* this penny, someone will give *you* more? You're stupid, Four Slots!"

"Well," Philip said quickly. "I-I thought it might start to . . . well . . ."

Philip blushed. Then he had a thought.

"Didn't you give your sister that doll out of the goodness of your heart?" Philip asked.

"You leave my sister out of this," Bradly blurted, leaning forward. "She didn't have anything to do with it."

"I know," Philip said.

"I didn't take it for me," Bradly explained.

"I know that too."

"Her old doll got burnt up in the fire," Bradly said in a softer voice. "Mom and Dad said they couldn't afford to buy her a new one."

Philip didn't know what to say. He just wanted to help.

"I started with a single penny too," he said, after Bradly had sniffed once or twice.

"Now you've got so much money you can give pennies away, huh?"

"I have more pennies, yeah," Philip admitted. "And I've learned a lot about how to get more and what to do with them once I have them. But I still have a lot to learn."

Bradly started to say something, then stopped and looked down. He seemed to become a bit calmer.

Philip thought Bradly looked like he was mentally wrestling with himself. When Bradly looked at Philip again, the mean look was gone from his face.

"Can I learn how to earn more pennies too?" Bradly asked.

Philip smiled. He reached into the pocket of his overalls and pulled out the last three pennies and handed them to Bradly.

"Sure," he said. "But you'll need your own blue notebook, to take notes about what you learn."

"Does it have to be blue?"

"It's my favorite color, but you can choose any color you want."

"Mine'll be green," Bradly said.

Philip laughed with Bradly as they walked to the stationery store, where Philip happened to know notebooks were on sale for three cents.

Philip realized in that moment that, if he had just made a new friend—never mind if he had stopped a bully—then he had already been rewarded tenfold for giving those pennies away.

Chapter 12

TRUE
WEALTH

S pring had sprung. Everywhere Philip looked, he saw new growth, including growth within himself.

Philip and his new friend Bradly were sitting on the hill behind Ms. Molly's orchard. The Big Red Book was open between them, pages fluttering from time to time in the soft spring breeze.

"You know," the Big Red Book said to Bradly. "If you're creating your own book, you should use your very best handwriting. It shows you care about your work. And a strong work ethic is very important."

"My writing's neat," Bradly protested, frowning at the book. "It's just as good as Philip's."

"Well, almost," Bradly grumbled.

The Big Red Book tilted its cover over Philip's notebook.

"Of course, Philip could be neater too," it said.

"Hey," Philip protested, pulling his book closer to hide his penmanship.

"The largest room in the world is the room for improvement," the Big Red Book announced.

Philip stuck out his tongue at Bradly, and they both laughed.

Suddenly, Philip could hear honking above them. He looked up and saw a flock of geese flying north. A goose wearing a backpack separated from the flock and flew down toward them.

"Hello there, young piglet," the goose said as he landed on the grass.

"George!" Philip shouted. "How was your trip south?"

"Too long," said a small voice from within George's backpack.

"Fantastic!" George said. "We wintered on a lovely Southern lake with incredible weather. And we didn't get lost once, thanks to you," he laughed.

"I'm so glad to see the weathervanes helped you."

"And I'm glad to see you two with your colorful notebooks."

"Do you know about these notebooks?" Philip asked, in surprise.

"You didn't think you were the only ones, did you?" George asked.

"Really!" said the voice from the backpack.

"Will you just . . ." George shrugged the pack off his back and reached inside. He pulled something out.

"You've got a Big Book too?!" Philip exclaimed.

"Well, I'm really more of a Little Book," the book interjected. "It makes me easier to travel with."

George nodded, and commented that his Little White Book reminded him of the white, puffy clouds he loved to pop in and out of.

"But it doesn't matter what size or color the book is," George said. "What matters is the beauty within."

"And I am loaded with that," the Little White Book said with a laugh.

"There are more of these books out there than you think," George said. "They have a way of finding their way into the possession of anyone who is willing to change their future by changing their thoughts, their habits, their actions, and therefore, their results."

"Just keep listening to that Big Red Book that found you," George said. "And writing your own," he added with a wink.

"Wait!" the little book cried. "I just got some fresh air. Don't stuff me back in that—"

The rest of its words were muffled by the pack.

"I'll see you in the fall!" George said, taking off into the bright blue sky.

Philip looked up. As he watched George catch up with his flock, he thought about how much things had changed. George knew how to get where he wanted to go, and in many ways, so did Philip.

He had the tools he needed to change his life.

He had friends and family to share that life with.

In his mind, Philip could picture all the animals he was going to help, and it filled his heart with joy.

This is wealth, he thought.

Then he and Bradly went back to work, mapping out their futures and dreaming big. Very big.

We are all special. We are all unique.
We all have things that make us neat.

Others may laugh. They may poke fun.
That is no reason to turn and run.

Stand in honor of your true self,
for your differences are your source of wealth.

In time you will see the truth in these words
and discover the greatness that you deserve.

Life is a journey, and it ebbs and it flows.
Be grateful for the happy and for the woes.

Take others by the hand, and teach them the same.
Always do your best, to represent your name.

You were not born to just fit in, but truly, to stand out.
Do your best. Have some fun. And smile.
For *that* is what life is all about.

ACKNOWLEDGEMENTS

Mom—For always being my biggest fan.

Dad—For always taking the time to know exactly how things are going.

Amy—It is our differences and experiences that make us unique and powerful.

Nana and Grampy—Nana, I know you're cheering from heaven. Grampy, ahhh-zing!

Nana Arbour—For your endless support.

Haleigh—Forever proud of you.

Harry Lanphear III—For your servant heart.

Connie Fotakis—For helping me build the "A-Team."

Dan Koon—For your hand in development.

Carrie Cook—Cookie! You're simply the best.

Amy Chamberlain—For making it shine.

Kalleheikki Kannisto—For your creative genius and bringing Philip to life.

Sara Jeanne—For your support and time providing valuable feedback.

Shellie Braeuner—For the splashes of magic.

Matt Stein—For thinking about all the things I did not.

Don Hutson—For teaching me about congruent intelligence.

Terri Murphy—For your ongoing hospitality.

Harvey Mackay—For teaching me about the largest room in the world.

Harvey Lipman—Go U Bears!

Miles Whitlock—Whose car we gonna take?

Devon Pcolar—Couldn't do it without you.

John Bridge—For giving it your all.

Clifford Jones—For clarity.